Dining
with the Danes

With Love from Bent And Betts
Hope you have Fun cooking
with this Danish book

Lynn Andersen

Dining with the Danes

Nyt Nordisk Forlag Arnold Busck

Dining with the Danes
©1996 by Nyt Nordisk Forlag Arnold Busck A/S
Typeset in Plantin and printed by Nørhaven Book, Viborg
3. oplag 2003
Printed in Denmark 2003

ISBN 87-17-06661-1

Editor: Anne Lisbeth Olsen
Design: Erik Nørskov
Photos: Jes Buusmann and John Roth Andersen

Acknowledgment
The author and the publishers wish to thank "The Federation of Danish Pig Producers and Slaughterhouses", "Danisco Distillers" and "Royal Greenland" for valuable cooperation and assistance, as well as for supplying us with their products for photography, and "Royal Copenhagen" and "Eva Trio" for lending us all the crockery used for photography.

About the author:
Lynn Andersen was born and grew up in Louisiana, USA. She has lived in Denmark for the past 25 years. She was trained at Suhrs Seminarium in Copenhagen and has written several cookbooks in Danish, such as: *Sund mad i wok, Cajun og kreolerkøkkenet*, and *Mad til tiden*. She is a food columnist at the Danish monthly magazine "I form".

Nyt Nordisk Forlag Arnold Busck
Købmagergade 49
1150 København K

www.nytnordiskforlag.dk   E:mail: nnf@nytnordiskforlag.dk

Contents

Meat

Foreword

When travelling in other countries, we try to eat the food that is traditional in each country. Therefore, we often have pleasant memories of certain places and of the food associated with those particular locations. To say that the Danes do not have a food culture, would be incorrect. The famous open faced sandwiches are unique. Denmark is the only place in the world where they can be found. Not even the other Scandinavian countries offer them. Also Danish pastry is famous. In some parts of the world, a pastry is simply called "a Danish".

The Danes, like all nationalities, have their traditions and their customs. Tourists who become tired of international menus in large, impersonal hotels, seek out the small, intimate restaurants where real Danish food is served.

Or they may visit Tivoli on a warm summer night. Here an important part of the fun is to taste the famous open faced sandwiches with freshly shelled shrimps piled high on white, buttered bread accompanied by a glass of ice cold aquavit (snaps).

Driving through the country side, stopping at a Danish inn to enjoy the special regional dishes that only the local cooks know how to prepare is also an enjoyable part of a visit to Denmark.

In this book I have tried to capture such pleasant memories of Denmark. The book contains some of the best known traditional dishes and a few of more modern dishes that you may have enjoyed while visiting the country.

Lynn Andersen

Conversion Table

1 kilogram (kilo) = 2 pounds (lb.)
1 pound (lb.) = 16 ounces (oz.)
1 ounce (oz.) = 30 grams (g)

Measures
1 quart = 1 liter
U.S. cup = 8 fluid ounces (fl.oz.)
1 British cup = 10 fluid ounces
(fl.oz.)

Teaspoon (tsp.) and tablespoon (tbsp.) are identical in American and British measurements. U.S. measurements for cup are used in this book.

Approximate oven temperatures

Centigrade	Fahrenheit
125-135	250-275
150-175	300-325
175-200	350-375
200-225	400-425
225-250	450-475

Soups

Golden, fertile fields, prosperous farms and an abundance of rivers running through the countryside, make Jutland a rich farmland. Today, the majority of Jutland is cultivated, but in the 19th century a great part of the area was covered by moorlands.

Chilled Tomato and Shrimp Soup

Serves 4

½ liter/16 fl.oz. chicken stock
4 tomatoes, skinned and chopped
½ cucumber, peeled and chopped
1 small onion, finely chopped

2 tbsp. red wine vinegar
white pepper
1 tsp. Dijon mustard
4 drops Tabasco sauce
350 g/12 oz. freshly shelled shrimps

Pour the stock into a serving bowl. Stir in the tomatoes, cucumber, onion, vinegar, pepper, mustard and Tabasco sauce. Add the shrimps and stir again. Cover the bowl and refrigerate for at least 1 hour. Serve in chilled soup bowls.

Asparagus Soup

Serves 4

1½ liters/2½ pints water
or unsalted chicken stock
1 kilo/2 lb. fresh asparagus,
   trimmed, cut into 2.5 cm
   (1 inch) pieces

30 g/1 oz. butter
3 tbsp. flour
2 egg yolks
salt and pepper

Cook the asparagus in water/chicken stock until they are tender, 10-12 minutes. Remove them with a slotted spoon. Cream the softened butter and flour, whisk it into the soup and boil for 5 minutes. Whisk the egg yolks with a little of the soup in a small bowl. Then pour it into the rest of the soup, stirring constantly. The soup must not boil after the egg is added or it will curdle. Add the asparagus pieces and heat them. Season with salt og pepper.

Cauliflower Soup

Serves 4

2 tbsp. butter
1 onion, chopped
2-3 carrots, finely chopped
1½ liter/2½ pints water or
   unsalted chicken stock

1 large (1 kilo/2 lb.) cauliflower,
   cut into small florets
½ cup/4 oz. cream
salt and pepper

Melt the butter in a large, heavy-bottomed saucepan over medium heat. Add the onions and carrots, and cook the mixture until the onions are translucent. Add the cauliflower florets and the water/stock. Boil for 5 minutes.

Remove the cauliflower florets and purée the rest in a blender or force through a sieve. Pour the mixture back into the saucepan and add the cream. Bring the soup to a boil and add the cauliflower florets. Season with salt and pepper.

Split Pea Soup with Salted Pork

Serves 6

500 g/1 lb. yellow split peas
4 sprigs of thyme
750 g/1½ lb. lightly salted lean
   pork
4-5 carrots, finely chopped
250 g/½ lb. celeriac, peeled and
   cut into 5 mm (¼ inch) cubes
3-4 leeks, trimmed, split and washed
   thoroughly to remove grit, and sliced

500 g/1 lb. potatoes, peeled, cut into
   2 cm (¾ inch) pieces
1 large onion, finely chopped
salt and pepper
500 g/1 lb. raw pork sausage

Put the peas into a pot with just enough water to cover. Add the thyme and boil the peas until they are tender; check the package as cooking time varies with the variety.

Remove the thyme and purée the peas in a blender or food processor.

Put the pork into another pot with just enough water to cover. Bring to a boil, skim off any impurities, then add salt. Simmer the meat for about 1½ hour. Add the vegetables when about 20 minutes of the cooking time remains. Add the sausage when 10 minutes are left.

Pour just enough broth from the meat into the peas to give them a suitable consistency - not too thin. Add the chopped vegetables and season to taste.

Slice the meat and serve with sausages on a plate. Serve the pea soup in a bowl.

Suggested accompaniment:
Rye bread, mustard and pickled beets.

Chicken Soup with Meatballs and Dumplings

1 large (1 kilo/2 lbs) hen/chicken
1 liter/2 pints water
½ celeriac, cut into chunks
4 carrots, chopped

5 leeks, washed thoroughly to remove all grit, and chopped bouquet garni of leek tops and a bunch of parsley

Meat Balls
250 g/½ lb. ground pork
250 g/½ lb. ground veal
2 tbsp. flour
¼ liter/8 fl. oz. milk
1 egg

Dumplings
150 g/6 oz. butter
150 g/6 oz. flour
5 eggs
¼ liter/8 fl. oz. milk

Bring the hen/chicken to a boil in a large pot with just enough water to cover. Skim and add vegetables, bouquet garni and salt. Remove the vegetables when they are tender. Continue cooking the hen until tender, about 1-2 hours. If the hen is very old, it will take up to 3-4 hours. Remove the hen and strain the soup.

To make the meatballs: Mix the ingredients together. Dip a teaspoon in boiling water and form a tiny ball in the palm of your hand. Drop the balls into boiling water as you make them. Cook them slowly for a few minutes, and remove from the water with a slotted spoon. Do not add to the soup until they are done, otherwise they will thicken the soup.

To make the dumplings: Melt the butter, stir in the flour and add 1 cup/8 oz. of boiling water. When the mixture is cool, add the eggs and a little salt. Form into tiny balls with a teaspoon, drop into boiling water, cook slowly for a few minutes, and remove from the water with a slotted spoon. Make sure the water doesn't boil.

Put the dumplings, the meat balls and the vegetables into the soup and serve.

Slice the hen/chicken and serve it0afterwards with asparagus sauce and boiled potatoes.

Asparagus Sauce

2 tbsp. butter
2 tbsp. flour
¼ liter/8 oz. of the
   chicken broth/stock

2 egg yolks
250 g/½ lb. asparagus

To make the asparagus sauce: melt the butter, stir in the flour and add the chicken broth a little at a time, stirring all the time. Add a little of the hot broth to the egg yolks and pour the mixture back into the broth. Do not let the sauce boil. Heat the asparagus gently in the sauce.

TIPS: The chicken broth and the chicken meat may also be used to make tartlets with creamed chicken (see page 66).

Oxtail Soup
Serves 4

1½ kilos/3 lb. oxtails, trimmed
   of all fat and cut into
   segments
60 g/2 oz. butter
1 onion, coarsely chopped
2-3 carrots, coarsely chopped
½ celeriac, sliced and cut
   into large chunks

2 liters/2 quarts water
salt and pepper
½-1 tbsp. paprika
2 tbsp. flour
sherry or madeira

Brown the oxtail pieces in butter in a large, heavy-bottomed pot over medium-high heat. Remove them and add the onion, carrots, celeriac, and leeks and brown them. Put the oxtail pieces back in the pot and add water. Bring to a boil, skim off the impurities and add the salt and paprika.

Cover and simmer for 2 hours. Remove the meat, strain and skim off the fat. Thicken the soup with flour and season with salt and pepper. A little dry sherry or madeira should be added just before serving.

The meat should be so tender that it falls from the bones. Add the meat to the soup in small pieces. The segments may be served in the soup or separately in a bowl.

Suggested accompaniment: Baguettes and hardboiled eggs.

Fish

Bornholm is Denmark's holiday island 132 kilometers east of the mainland. Here you can find cliffs, forests, beaches and have hours of fun. It is also the home of the famous smoked herring. There are so many fish that one could scoop them up in a bucket.

Salmon with Lemon Vinaigrette and Horseradish Dressing

Serves 8

1½ kilos/3 lb. salmon fillet, with the skin left on

Marinade	*Dressing*
6 lemons	1 cup/8 oz. sour cream
salt	2 cups/16 fl.oz. heavy cream,
freshly ground white pepper	whipped
lettuce leaves	2 tbsp. lemon juice
cress and lemon wedges	salt
for garnish	freshly ground white pepper
	2 tbsp. freshly grated horseradish

Carefully remove all the bones. Grate the rind of two of the lemons. Squeeze the juice from all six lemons and add it to the rind. Place the salmon in a deep dish and pour the lemon mixture over. Sprinkle with salt and freshly ground white pepper. Cover and refrigerate for at least 4 hours. Make sure the salmon is covered with lemon juice or turn the fillet once or twice while marinating.

Whisk together all the ingredients for the dressing in a bowl. Cut the salmon in very thin slices diagonally across the grain.

Decorate a platter with finely shredded iceberg lettuce and place the salmon slices on top. Decorate with lemon wedges and cress. Serve the dressing on the side.

Danish Caviar

Lumpfish roe is sold fresh in the fish shops of Denmark during the spring months, and in jars over most of the world all year round. It is available in its own natural color, but can also be brought with black and red food coloring added so that it resembles real caviar from the sturgeon.

It can be used as a first course served with toasted bread, lemon wedges and sour cream. It is often used as a garnish for fish, such as fried plaice, and other sandwiches.

If you are lucky enough to get hold of fresh roe, here is how to prepare it. Open the sac and press the roe out into a bowl. Remove the largest membranes. Pour cold water over and with an electric mixer, beat the roe. Let stand for 5 minutes.

Pour off the impurities that have floated to the surface. Repeat this process. Drain the roe and season with salt, pepper and lemon juice. Add 1 cup/8 oz. finely chopped onion if the roe is to be served plain with toast and sour cream.

Omelette with Smoked Herring - as a luncheon dish

Serves 4

8 eggs	2-3 tomatoes, sliced in wedges
8 tbsp. milk	a large bunch of radishes,
salt and pepper	thinly sliced
butter for frying	a large bunch of chives, finely
2-3 smoked herrings	chopped
(usually canned, if not	
available fresh)	

In a bowl, whisk together the eggs, milk, salt and pepper. Melt the butter in a large frying pan over medium heat. Pour the mixture into the pan and let it cook slowly until it is firm and the bottom and sides are browned - about 8 minutes.

Arrange the herring fillets in a star on top of the omelette just before it is set. Arrange the tomato wedges and sliced radishes along the edge of the pan. Sprinkle with plenty of chopped chives. Serve the omelette in the pan immediately.

Suggested accompaniment: Wholemeal bread

TIPS: Slices of bacon or lightly salted lean pork can be placed on the omelette instead of smoked herring (see page 42).

Asparagus and Smoked Salmon - as a first course

Wrap 1-2 slices of smoked salmon around 2 pieces of freshly cooked asparagus and serve with baguettes as a first course.

Smoked Salmon with Creamed Spinach
Serves 4

4-8 slices of smoked salmon
Creamed Spinach:
1 kilo/2 lb. fresh spinach,
    stems removed, washed or
    500 g/1 lb. frozen

1 tbsp. butter
½ cup/4 fl.oz. heavy cream
salt and white pepper

Cook the spinach with just the water that clings from its washing. When the spinach has shrunk, turn it on to a plate, let it cool and chop it coarsely with a knife. Melt the butter in a small casserole and put the spinach, cream, salt and pepper in. Cook the spinach over medium heat for 5 minutes.

Arrange the slices of salmon decoratively on a platter and serve the creamed spinach in a bowl by itself. Or, arrange 1-2 slices of salmon on four individual plates and place a large scoop of spinach next to it.

TIPS: Scrambled eggs may also be served with smoked salmon as well as with freshly cooked asparagus. Wrap the slices of salmon decoratively around 2-3 freshly cooked asparagus. They may be tied nicely with the blanched green stems of spring onions or long chives.

Marinated Salmon (Sugar-Salted Dill Salmon)

1 kilo/2 lb. salmon fillet, bones
  removed, with the skin on
2 tbsp. salt
2 tbsp. sugar

1½ tsp. crushed white pepper
6 tbsp. rinsed and finely cut fresh
  dill

As this salmon is not cooked, only the freshest possible fish should be used. Rinse the fish under cold running water and pat dry with paper towels. Cut the salmon into two fillets.

Combine the salt, sugar and pepper in a bowl. Rub the flesh side of the fish with this mixture.

Sprinkle 2 tbsp. of dill on a platter and place one of the fillets, skin side down on it. Sprinkle 2 tbsp. of dill on top. Place the other fillet, flesh side down, on the first filet. Sprinkle with the rest of the dill. Now, cover with a heavy article weighing 1-1½ kilos/2-3 lb. Chill the salmon in the refrigerator 24 hours. Turn the fillets 2-3 times. The skin should always be on the outside.

Scrape the dill off. With a sharp, thin-bladed (filleting) knife cut the fish in oblong squares of 10-15 cm/4-6 in. Remove any bones left and cut the meat into thin slices from one side of the fillet to the other until you reach the skin.

Mustard-Dill Sauce

1 tbsp. sweet mustard
1 tbsp. sour mustard
½ cup/4 fl.oz. oil

2-3 tbsp. vinegar
3-4 tbsp. fresh, finely chopped dill

Whisk all the ingredients together in a small bowl. Check the seasoning. You can add a little sugar if it is too sour.

Luncheon Plate with Marinated Salmon and Smoked Salmon

Arrange 2-3 slices each of marinated salmon and smoked salmon attractively on a plate, decorate with a sprig of dill and some lemon wedges. Serve mustard-dill dressing and sourdough or white bread on the side. This way the guests may take as much or as little dressing as they wish.

Tartlets with Creamed Fish

Serves 6

175 g/6 oz. flour
90 g/3 oz. butter
1 egg

Filling
200 g/7 oz. shrimps
250 g/8 oz. canned asparagus tips
1 cup/8 fl.oz. asparagus liquid
½ cup/4 fl.oz. cream
3 tbsp. butter
2 tbsp. flour
salt and pepper
dill

Sift the flour into a mixing bowl. Add the butter and rub it into the flour with your fingertips until the mixture resembles fine breadcrumbs. Add the egg and form a dough. Knead briefly on a ligthy floured surface until smooth; do not overwork the dough or it will become oily and the baked pastry will be tough.

On a lightly floured surface, roll out the dough to a thickness of 5mm/¼ inch. Cut out 12 circles with a glass and use them to line 6 cm/2½ inch deep tartlet tins. Prick the insides with a fork, then chill the tartlet cases for 30 minutes.

Preheat the oven to 220°C.

Arrange the tartlet cases on a baking sheet and bake 5 minutes.

Filling:
Bring the cream and asparagus liquid to a boil. Cream the butter and flour and whisk the mixture into the liquid. Boil 2-3 minutes. Warm the shrimps and asparagus tips in the sauce. Fill the warm tartlets with this filling and garnish with dill sprigs.

West Coast Seafood Salad

Serves 4

250 g/8 oz. mixed salad greens,
    washed and dried
200 g/7 oz. freshly shelled
    shrimps
500 g/1 lb. peas, shelled or
150 g/5 oz. frozen peas, thawed

Dressing
½ cup/4 fl.oz. oil
2 tbsp. vinegar or lemon juice
salt and pepper
½ tsp. sour mustard

Toss the salad greens with the shrimps and peas. Whisk ingredients for the dressing together and pour over the salad just before serving.
Serve with baguettes.

Shooting Star

Serves 4

4 fried plaice (see below),
    with the skin removed
200 g/7 oz. shelled shrimps

200 g/7 oz. asparagus tips
lemon wedges
chopped fresh dill

Just before serving the fried plaice, place a line of shrimps along the middle of the fish. On each side of the shrimps, arrange a row of asparagus tips. Add a wedge or two of lemon and sprinkle with finely chopped fresh dill.

Serve with either browned butter or a light white wine sauce.

Fried Plaice

Serves 4

4 fresh plaice, with the skin
   removed
3-4 tbsp. flour/dried bread
   crumbs,

finely crumbled
salt and pepper
60 g/2 oz. butter
1 lemon

Rinse, pat dry and dredge the fish in a mixture of flour, salt and pepper. Fry the fish in a large frying pan two at a time in slightly browned butter over medium heat. Serve with small new potatoes sprinkled with finely chopped parsley, melted butter and lemon wedges.

Homemade remoulade is the accompaniment most Danes prefer.

Homemade Remoulade

75 g/2½ oz. mayonnaise
2 tbsp. plain yoghurt
2 tbsp. chopped pickles
1 very small onion, finely
   chopped

1 tbsp. capers
1 tbsp. finely chopped parsley
a few drops lemon juice
salt

Blend the mayonnaise with the yoghurt and mix the rest of the ingredients into the mayonnaise mixture.

Plaice with Shrimps and Asparagus

Serves 4

4 large or 8 small fillet of plaice
1 cup/8 fl.oz. fish stock
½ cup/4 fl.oz. white wine
15 g/½ oz. butter
1 ½ tbsp. flour

½ cup/4 oz. heavy cream
250 g/8 oz.freshly shelled shrimps
250 g/8 oz. freshly cooked
   asparagus tips

With the skinned side on the inside, fold each fillet neatly into three. Place them in a shallow saucepan in a single layer, then pour in the fish stock. Cover the saucepan and simmer the fillets for 5-6 minutes, until they are just cooked.

With a slotted spoon, carefully lift the fillets from the saucepan and arrange them on a warm serving dish. Cover and keep warm while making the sauce.

Boil the fish stock rapidly until it is reduced to half, then add the white wine. Blend the butter and flour together to make a smooth paste. Whisk the butter into the stock and bring to a boil. Reduce the heat to low and simmer 3-4 minutes.

Stir in the cream and heat for 1 minute without boiling. Spoon the sauce over the fish and place the shrimps along the center of the dish. Place the asparagus tips next to the shrimps.

Suggested accompaniment:
Creamed spinach (see page 25) or creamed mushrooms.

Fried Garfish Filled with Parsley

Serves 4

2 (1½ kilos/3 lb.) fresh garfish	½ cup/4 oz. dried bread crumbs
2 bunches of parsley	salt and pepper
1 egg	butter for frying

Clean, bone and halve the garfish, cutting the fillets into two halves. There should be 8 pieces. Roll a sprig of parsley inside each fillet and fasten with a toothpick. Dip the fish in beaten egg and roll it in dried bread crumbs (see page 86). Brown the butter in a frying pan over high heat, and sauté the garfish until golden brown all over. Reduce the temperature and allow to simmer over a low heat for about 5 minutes. Remove the fish from the pan and keep hot while melting more butter.

Serve with boiled potatoes and green salad. Serve the melted butter in a separate bowl.

Fried Eel with Creamed Potatoes

Serves 4

1-2 kilos/2-4 lb. eels,
   gutted and skinned
salt and pepper

4-5 tbsp. flour
60 g/2 oz. butter

Creamed Potatoes

1½ kilos/3 lb. boiled potatoes
3 tbsp. butter
3 tbsp. flour

approx. ½ liter/16 fl.oz. milk
salt and pepper
chives

Rinse and dry the eels carefully. Cut them into 3 inch pieces, sprinkle with salt, rinse and dry thoroughly. Roll them in flour and brown them in butter over high heat. Turn down the heat and fry 15-30 minutes depending on how thick they are.

Creamed potatoes: Dice the potatoes. Melt the butter and stir in the flour. Dilute with milk, stirring all the time. Boil the mixture for 5 minutes before adding the diced potatoes. Season with salt and pepper. Sprinkle with lots of chopped chives just before serving.

Boiled Cod

Serves 4

2 kilos/4 lb. cod or one large piece
Stock per liter of water:
1 tbsp. salt
4-5 whole peppercorns
2 bay leaves

Accompaniments:
125 g/5 oz. butter
fish mustard
chopped hard-boiled eggs
pickled beets (see page 33)

Rinse the fish under cold running water. Cut off the fins and discard them. Scale the fish and remove the black membrane inside the white bladder.

Place in a fish kettle or pan large enough to accommodate the cod. Add enough water to just cover the fish. Add the salt, peppercorns, and bay leaves. Bring the fish slowly to a boil. Skim the stock and simmer the fish gently for 15-20 minutes. The water should just bubble at the edges. Remove the fish with a slotted spoon and place it on a heated platter.

Fish mustard sauce:
Melt 30 g/1 oz. of butter in a saucepan, stir in 1 tbsp. of flour and add the fish stock stirring all the time. Add a little milk or cream, a tbsp. of the special fish mustard and let the sauce simmer 2-3 minutes. Season with salt and white pepper.

Serve with butter, fish mustard sauce, chopped hard-boiled eggs, pickled beets and boiled potatoes.

Pickled Red Beets

1 kilo/1 lb red beets
150-250 g/5 oz-8oz. sugar
½ liter/16 fl.oz. vinegar

Clean the beets and boil in water until tender - about one hour. Test with a knitting needle. Pour off the water and skin them while they are warm. Allow to cool, then slice and place them in a clean glas jar. Bring the vinegar and sugar to a boil. Pour the boiling liquid over the beets, covering them completely. After 24 hours they are ready to serve. Pickled beets are used to garnish and accompany many types of sandwiches, as well as meatballs and sausages.

Poached Halibut in Orange-Lemon Sauce

Serves 4

500 g/1 lb. halibut fillets, rinsed
   and patted dry
1 cup/8 fl.oz. fish stock/water
1 cup/8 fl.oz. dry white wine
½ cup fresh orange juice
1 tbsp. fresh lemon juice
2 shallots, finely chopped

1 tbsp. fresh thyme, or 1 tsp. dried
   freshly ground black pepper
30 g/1 oz. butter
1 large lettuce (about 150 g/5 oz.),
   cored and washed
½ tsp. salt

To prepare the poaching liquid, combine the fish stock, white wine, orange juice, lemon juice, half of the chopped shallots, half of the thyme and some black pepper in a large pan. Bring the liquid to the boil, then reduce the heat to medium low. Allow to simmer for 10 minutes.

Cut the fillets diagonally in half. Place the thicker fillets in the simmering liquid and poach them gently for 1 minute. Add the thinner fillets and continue poaching until the fish is opaque and feels firm to the touch, 3-4 minutes. Remove the fish to a plate and keep warm.

Sauce: Raise the heat to medium and simmer the poaching liquid until it is reduced to about ½ cup/4 fl.oz. Strain the sauce through a sieve into a small pan and set aside.

Melt half of the butter in the same pan over medium heat. Add the remaining shallots and thyme, and cook for 1 minute, stirring. Add the lettuce leaves, some salt and some pepper and keep stirring, until the lettuce has wilted - 2 minutes. Place the lettuce on a warm serving plate.

Reheat the sauce; stir in the remaining salt and whisk in the remaining butter. Place the fish pieces on the wilted lettuce, pour the sauce over the fish and serve.

Suggested accompaniment: Steamed courgettes with diced sweet red pepper.

Fish Cakes

Serves 4

500 g/1 lb. fillet of cod	½ cup/4 oz. milk
1 onion, peeled and finely chopped	½ cup/4 oz. light cream
4 tbsp. flour	1 tsp. salt
2 eggs	a dash of white pepper
	fat for frying

Cut the fish into small pieces and chop it with a sharp knife until the fish is minced as coarsely or finely as you like. (You can put it through a meat grinder together with the chopped onion, but it will be very fine). Mix the onion and flour with the fish and add the eggs. Stir in the milk and cream a little at a time. Season with salt and pepper.

Melt the fat in a frying pan. Dip a soup spoon in the fat, before taking a scoop of the mixture. Shape the mixture into a flattened ball or cake in the palm of your hand. Place the cakes in the pan as you make them. Fry over low heat for 5 minutes and make sure that they do not get crusty too quickly.

Serve with lemon wedges, boiled potatoes, and remoulade (see page 30).

Whole Poached Salmon

Serves 8

2 kilos/4 lb. whole salmon, gutted	3 sprigs fresh thyme, or 1 tsp. dried
3 liters/5 pints water	2 bay leaves
2 onions, thinly sliced	5 peppercorns, cracked
2 carrots, peeled and thinly sliced	1½ cup/12 fl.oz. white wine
10 parsley stems	

Put the onions, carrots, parsley, thyme, bay leaves and pepper-corns in a large pot with the water. Bring the liquid to a boil. Reduce the heat and simmer the liquid, with the lid slightly ajar, for 15 minutes.

Add the wine and simmer for another 15 minutes. Strain the liquid through a fine sieve into a bowl before using it.

Wash the salmon inside and out under cold running water. Pour the stock into a fish kettle* or pan large enough to accommodate the salmon. Place the fish into the fish kettle. Bring the liquid to a simmer over medium heat. Cover the pan, reduce the heat to low, and cook the salmon for 8 minutes per 2.5 cm (1 inch) of thickness (measured at its thickest point).

Let the fish cool in the liquid, then carefully transfer it to a work surface. Make a long cut along the back and the belly of the salmon. Then working from the base of the tail towards the head, gently pull off the skin in strips.

Carefully transfer the fish to a long platter, placing it skinned side down. Remove the skin from the second side.

Serve the salmon warm with hollandaise sauce or cold with mayonnaise, freshly shelled shrimps and lobster tails.

* If you do not have a fish kettle or pot large enough for the salmon, it can be cooked in the oven at 200°C. If the fish is too large to handle, it can be wrapped in a piece of muslin that is about 25 cm (10 inches) longer than the fish. Knot each end of the muslin and secure it by tying string around the fish in two or three places. This way, the knotted ends of the cloth can be used to lift the fish into and out of the liquid.

Fried Herring

Serves 4

4 large or 8 small herrings	*Vinegar Dressing*
4 tbsp. flour	1 cup/8 fl.oz. vinegar
salt and pepper	¼ cup/2 fl.oz. water
butter for frying	4 tbsp. sugar
	2 bay leaves
	a sprig of thyme
	6 coarsely crushed peppercorns

Wash the herrings thoroughly, then pat them dry with paper towels. To remove the bones, take one fish at a time and place it on a work surface belly down. Gently, but firmly, press along the length of the backbone to flatten the fish. Turn the herring over, and run a thumb under the bones at each side of the backbone to loosen. Lift the bones out in one piece and snip the backbone 2.5 cm (1 inch) from the tail. Cut shallow diagonal slashes at 2.5 cm (1 inch) intervals along the sides of each fish.

Dredge the herrings in a mixture of flour and salt and pepper. Heat the butter until golden and fry the herrings 4-5 minutes, depending on the thickness.

Dressing: Boil the vinegar, water, sugar, bay leaves, thyme and peppercorns 5 minutes over low heat. Cool the marinade before pouring it over the warm herrings.

Refrigerate until the following day. Garnish with plenty of raw onions rings.

Meat

Just an hour's drive from the capital, in the northern part of Zealand, lies the famous Hamlet's Kronborg Castle. The road to the castle is known as the Danish Riviera with many beautiful homes by the seaside and old village inns encouraging both Danes and tourists alike to stop for coffee and pastry. Better yet, stopping and enjoying a picnic on the beach in front of the castle, while watching ships sail to and from Sweden is also a favourite pass time.

Pork

Pork Roast with Crackling

Serves 6

(In Denmark this dish is usually roasted with the rind on.)

1 ½ kilos/3 lb. boned pork
   loin with the rind
1 ½ tbsp. salt
2-3 bay leaves
¾ liter/1 ¼ pints water

Gravy
½ liter/16 fl.oz. broth and
pan juices
½ cup/4 oz. cream
flour for thickening
gravy browning or caramel color
salt and pepper

Ask your butcher to make parallel slits in the rind, without cutting into the meat itself. Rub the meat thoroughly with salt, making sure the salt gets down into the slits in the rind. Place the bay leaves in the slits. Put the roast on a rack in a baking pan. The roast should be as level as possible. Use foil, if necessary, to prop up the roast. Pour the water into the pan. Place the roast in a cold oven and turn on the oven to 200°C. After 1 ½ hours the roast should have a temperature of 65°C. Pour the pan juices off and save them for the gravy. If the rind is not sufficiently crisp, brown the roast, either by using the grill or by turning the heat up to 225°C.

Let the uncovered roast rest in a warm place 20 minutes. The internal temperature should read 70°C.

Gravy: Skim off the fat from the pan juices and strain the juices. Pour into a saucepan and dilute with bouillon or stock, making ¾ liter/1 ¼ pints in all. Add cream and bring to a boil. Thicken with flour and season with salt and pepper.

Slice the roast and serve with glazed potatoes, red cabbage (see page 42), cooked apple halves filled with a dab of red jelly.

Glazed Potatoes

Serves 4

1 kilo/2 lb. small potatoes, boiled and peeled	90 g/3 oz. sugar
	75 g/2 oz. butter

Melt the sugar on a frying pan until golden. Add the butter. Glaze and brown the potatoes in the caramelized sugar, turning constantly.

Cooked Apples Stuffed with Prunes

Serves 4-8

225 g/8 oz. sugar	8 large apples, cored and peeled
portwine to taste	1 liter/1½ pints cold water
16 prunes	

Put 2 tbsp. sugar, the port and prunes into an ovenproof dish. Leave to marinate 6-8 hours.

Preheat the oven to 170°C. Place the prunes in the oven and cook for 20-30 minutes or until soft.

Cut the apples in half. Mix the remaining sugar and water in a pan and boil for 2-3 minutes. Add the apples and leave to simmer for 10 minutes uncovered, over a low heat. Remove the apples with a slotted spoon and place in a serving dish. Put one prune on each apple half.

These apples are used to accompany pork roast with crackling, meat loaf and roast duck, if the duck has not been stuffed with prunes and apples.

Stewed Red Cabbage

Serves 4

1 kilo/2 lb. red cabbage,
(outer leaves removed),
finely chopped
2-4 tbsp. butter

2 tbsp. sugar
2 tbsp. wine vinegar
1 cup/8 fl.oz. red currant juice
salt

Melt butter and sugar in a heavy bottomed saucepan, add the cabbage, steam slightly, then add a little water and the vinegar.

Cover and simmer 60 minutes. Stir occasionally. When nearly done, add red currant juice and more sugar and vinegar to taste. Red cabbage is best, if prepared the day, before it is to be used. Serve with roast pork or roast duck.

Omelette with Fried Pork

Serves 4

400 g/¾ lb. lightly salted
pork or bacon
8 eggs
8 tbsp. milk

salt and pepper
butter for frying
a large bunch of chives

Cut the pork into slices. Fry without fat on a hot frying pan, until the slices are golden and tender.

Whisk together the eggs, milk, salt and pepper in a bowl. Melt the butter in a large frying pan over medium heat. Pour the egg mixture into the pan and let it cook slowly, until it is firm and the bottom and sides are browned - about 8 minutes. Arrange the fried pork slices on top of the omelette just before it sets. Sprinkle with plenty of clipped chives.

Christmas Ham

Serves 10-12

3-4 kilos/6-8 lb. lightly salted, smoked ham

for the glaze:	1 tbsp. brown sugar
1 egg yolk	2 tbsp. dried bread crumbs
2 tbsp. mustard	(see page 86)

Dry the ham with a paper towel. Insert a thermometer at the thickest place. Place the ham in a cold oven and bake it, until the thermometer shows 65°C-70°C, 2-2½ hours.

Remove the thermometer and increase the temperature to 225°C. Skin the ham, leaving the fat on. Mix the egg yolk and mustard and spread over the fat. Mix the sugar with the bread crumbs and sprinkle over the ham. Return the ham to the oven and bake until the breadcrumbs are slightly browned.
The ham can be eaten warm or cold.

Suggested accompaniment: Cooked apple slices and prunes, stewed cabbage, creamed spinach (see page 25) or a fresh vegetable.

Burning Love

Serves 4

1½ kilos/3 lb. potatoes, peeled and cut into 2.5 cm (1 inch) cubes	1 kilo/2 lb. lightly salted, smoked lean pork, cut into 2.5 cm (1 inch) cubes
1½ cups/12 oz. milk	2 large onions, sliced
30 g/1 oz. butter	parsley, finely chopped
salt and pepper	

Boil the potatoes in unsalted water. Fry the pork in a frying pan. Remove the meat and fry the onions in the remaining fat.

Mash the potatoes and beat in the milk and butter until fluffy. Season to taste with salt and pepper.

Place the mashed potatoes on a serving platter and top with the pork cubes and onions. Sprinkle with chopped parsley before serving.

Meat Loaf

Serves 6

1 kilo/2 lb. ground pork	2 tbsp. grated onion
3 tbsp. dried bread crumbs	4-6 tbsp. chicken stock
(see page 86)	8 thin slices of bacon
½ tsp. pepper	1 cup/8 fl.oz. stock
½ tsp. ground ginger	½ cup/4 fl.oz. heavy cream
½ tsp. mustard powder	red currant or rowanberry jelly
1 egg	

Preheat the oven to 225°C.

Mix the ground pork with the bread crumbs, the spices, egg, onion and 4-6 tablespoons of the chicken stock.

Shape the meat into an oblong loaf and put it in a greased baking dish. Cover with the bacon slices.

Brown the loaf for 15 minutes. Reduce the temperature to 170°C and pour the stock and the cream over the meat. Roast for another 40-45 minutes.

Pour the drippings into a saucepan and bring to a boil.

Season the sauce with a little fruit jelly, 1-2 tablespoons - and salt and pepper. If the sauce is too pale, add gravy coloring.

Suggested accompaniment: Hasselback potatoes, applesauce and jelly.

Hasselback Potatoes

Make as many potatoes as the family can eat, 1-2 per person. Peel the potatoes and cut them i thin slices ⅔ of the way through. Brush them with oil and sprinkle with coarse salt. Place them in the oven next to the meat loaf. If they are not too large, they should be ready when the meat loaf is done.

Danish Meatballs

Serves 4

500 g/1 lb. ground pork
5 tbsp. flour
1 egg
1 medium grated onion

1 cup/8 fl.oz. milk,
soda water or stock
salt and pepper
butter for frying

Combine the ground meat with the flour and egg and mix in the grated onion. Add the liquid a little at a time, mixing well. Add salt and pepper. Let the mixture rest for half an hour to see if more liquid should be added.

Melt the butter in a frying pan until golden. It is important that the pan is very hot, before the meatballs are put in or they will stick to the pan. Dip a soup spoon in the fat, and afterwards dip the spoon into the mixture, forming a "round" meatball. Drop the meatballs into the fat. Scoop a little of the fat over each meatball. Reduce the heat and fry the meatballs 6 minutes, then turn them over. Fry them 6 minutes on the other side.

Suggested accompaniments: Creamed cabbage and potatoes

Creamed White Cabbage

Serves 4

1 kilo/2 lb. white cabbage,
   (outer leaves removed),
   finely chopped
3 tbsp. flour

3 tbsp. butter
½ liter/16 fl.oz. milk
salt and pepper

Cook the cabbage in salted water until tender. Remove from the heat and drain.

Make a white sauce of melted butter and flour, and enough milk to make a smooth, thin sauce. Add the cooked cabbage and season with salt and pepper.

Pork and Brown Cabbage

Serves 4

2 tbsp. sugar
2 tbsp. butter
1½ kilos/3 lb. head of white
   cabbage, (outer leaves removed),
   coarsely chopped

1 kilo/2 lb. pork spare-ribs, fresh
   or slightly salted

Caramelize the sugar in a heavy bottomed pot over a low heat. Add the butter and brown the cabbage in this. If a darker color is desired, add a little soy sauce. Add a little water - about 1 cup/8 oz. and the pork, cover and steam until tender - about 1 hour.

The pork can be cut into smaller pieces, in which case it should not be added until about 35 minute before the cabbage is done.

Pork Loin with Apples and Prunes

Serves 4

1 kilo/2 lb. boned pork loin,
   trimmed of fat
15-20 pitted prunes
2-3 cooking apples, quartered,
   and cored, cut into 8 wedges

salt and pepper
30 g/1 oz. butter
1 cup/8 fl.oz. water
1-2 tbsp. flour

Cut a lengthwise slit about half way into the pork loin, and flatten it by beating it lightly. Spread prunes and apples over the flattened surface, fold the meat and tie with string in six or eight places. Rub with salt and pepper and brown quickly in the melted butter. Add water and cook the meat for ¾ to 1 hour. Skim off fat and thicken with a little flour. Add a few drops of gravy browning for additional color.

Suggested accompaniment: Mashed parsnips (page 50)

Mashed Parsnips

Serves 4

1 kilo/2 lb. parsnips peeled and cut into small pieces	approx. 1½ liters water
250 g/½ lb. potatoes, peeled and cut into small pieces	½ cup/4 fl.oz. heavy cream
	salt, pepper
	fresh thyme leaves

Cover the parsnips and potatoes with water. Bring to a boil, and cook until tender, 15-20 minutes. Drain the liquid and save it.

With a mixer at low speed, beat the parsnips and potatoes, adding the water and the cream a little at a time. Beating at medium speed, continue for 2-4 minutes until mixture is smooth. Season with salt, pepper and thyme leaves.

Fried Pork with Parsley Sauce

Serves 4

600 g/1¼ lb. lightly salted, smoked pork

Parsley sauce	1½ cup/12 oz. milk
3 tbsp. butter	a bunch of parsley
2 tbsp. flour	salt and pepper

Cut the pork in slices. Fry the pork without fat in a hot frying pan until the slices are golden and tender.

Sauce:
Melt the butter in a saucepan and stir in the flour. Dilute with milk. Boil for a few minutes before adding the freshly chopped parsley. Season to taste with salt and pepper.

Suggested accompaniment: Boiled potatoes.

Fried Pork with Apples

Serves 4

8 slices bacon
  or slightly salted pork

1 kilo/2 lb. cooking apples,
  quartered, and cored,
  cut into 8 wedges
sugar to taste

Fry the pork without fat in a hot frying pan until the slices are golden brown and tender, remove them and keep hot in a covered dish.

Fry the apples in the pork fat until they are soft, but not mushy, turn them with care.

When the apples are done, add sugar to taste and put them in a hot dish with pork slices placed decoratively on top.

Suggested accompaniment: Boiled potatoes with finely chopped parsley, or dark rye bread (see page 92)

There are many farmers in Denmark and the country side is dot-
ted with old villages. Fåborg provides a charming example. The
Danes eat more meat than other Scandinavians and produce large
amounts for export. Many farms raise both cattle and pigs as a
major source of income.

Beef

Sailor's Stew

Serves 6

1 kilo/2 lb. lean beef or veal,
cut in 5 cm/2 inch chunks
5 large onions, coarsely chopped
90 g/3 oz. butter
12 whole peppercorns

2 bay leaves
1½ kilos/3 lb. potatoes, diced
butter
a bunch of parsley, finely chopped

Melt the butter in a heavy bottomed pot and toss the meat and onions in the butter, but do not brown them. Add boiling water until the meat is just covered, then add a pinch of salt, the peppercorns, and the bay leaves. Simmer over low heat for about 20 minutes. Add the diced potatoes and let the mixture cook until the potatoes have been blended with the meat broth, giving the appearance of a very thick potato soup. Remove from the heat and place a large pat of butter in the center.

Sprinkle with finely chopped parsley and place a dish with small balls of butter on the table so that each portion can be topped with a butter ball.

Suggested accompaniment: Dark rye bread or wholemeal bread

Salted Brisket of Beef with Spring Cabbage

Serves 4

2 kilos/4 lb. lightly salted
brisket of beef
1 spring cabbage, core removed,
cut into 4-5 wedges
3 tbsp. butter

3 tbsp. flour
1½ cup/12 fl.oz. cabbage water
1½ cup/12 fl.oz. milk
salt and white pepper
1 tsp. ground nutmeg

Cover the brisket with water and cook until tender, about 2 hours. Cook the cabbage in lightly salted water for 15 minutes.

Melt the butter and stir in the flour. Add the cabbage water and milk a little at a time. Bring the mixture to a boil and season with salt, pepper and ground nutmeg. Chop the cabbage coarsely and add it to the creamed sauce.

Carve the brisket and arrange the slices on a warmed serving platter. Spoon some of the sauce over the slices and place the remaining cabbage in a bowl.

Roast Beef with Mushroom Sauce

Serves 6-8

1½ kilos/3 lb. boned and rolled sirloin, trimmed of fat
4 tbsp. freshly ground pepper
2½ tbsp. mustard
2 tbsp. plain yoghurt
2 tbsp. butter
250 g/8 oz. mushrooms, wiped clean and quartered
40 g/1½ oz. shallots or onion, thinly sliced

1 tbsp. chopped fresh rosemary, or 1 tsp. dried
1 cup/8 fl.oz. red wine
1 garlic clove, finely chopped
½ liter/16 fl.oz. unsalted brown or chicken stock
½ tsp. salt
½ cup/4 oz. heavy cream

Preheat the oven to 240°C.

Spread the ground pepper on a plate. Mix 2 tablespoons of the mustard with the yoghurt and smear this mixture over the beef. Roll the beef in the pepper, coating it evenly on all sides.

Place the beef on a rack set in a roasting pan. For medium-rare meat, cook the roast until a meat thermometer inserted in the center registers 60°C (140°F) - about 35 minutes. Let the roast rest while the mushroom sauce is prepared.

Sauce: Melt the butter and add the mushrooms, shallots/onions, and rosemary, and cook them, stirring often, for 5 minutes. Add the wine and the garlic, rapidly boil the liquid until it is reduced by half - about 3 minutes. Stir in the stock and salt, reduce the sauce once again until only about 1½ cup/½ pint of liquid remains. Whisk in the cream together with the remaining mustard. Simmer the sauce for a few minutes to thicken it.

To serve, carve the roast into very thin slices. Arrange the slices on a serving platter and pour over the mushroom sauce.

Suggested accompaniment: Scorzonera with mixed herbs (see page 56)

Danish Hash

Serves 4

400 g/¾ lb. cold beef or pork,
  diced
4 tbsp. butter
500 g/1 lb. boiled potatoes, diced
2 large onions, coarsely chopped

salt and pepper
Worcestershire sauce or
  tomato catsup
1 fried egg for each person

Brown the meat in butter in a frying pan. Remove the meat and set aside. Brown the potatoes in butter. Remove them and mix with the meat. Brown the onions in butter and return txe meat and potatoes to the frying pan. Heat well, season with salt and pepper. Serve garnished with fried egg. Offer Worcesterhire sauce or tomato catsup.

Oxtail Ragout

Serves 6

2 oxtails 1½-2 kilos/3-4 lb.
  trimmed of all fat
  and cut into segments
2-3 tbsp. flour
4-5 tbsp. butter
2 large onions, sliced
3 tsp. paprika
3 tbsp. tomato paste

½ liter/16 fl.oz. stock/bouillon
2 bay leaves
2 sprigs of thyme
4 carrots, chopped
½ celeriac, sliced and cut into
  large chunks
4 leeks, washed thoroughly to
  remove all grit, and sliced

Dredge the oxtail pieces in flour and brown them in the butter in a large, heavy-bottomed pot over medium-high heat. Add the onions and brown them. Add the paprika and tomato paste, diluted with a little bouillon. Add the rest of the liquid and the herbs. Cover and simmer for 1 hour. Add the vegetables and cook until the meat and vegetables are tender. The meat should be so tender that it falls from the bones. Season to taste with salt and pepper. A little dry sherry can be added just before serving.

Suggested accompaniment: Mashed potatoes

Scorzonera with Mixed Herbs

Serves 6

750 g/1½ lb. scorzonera,
   scrubbed well
1 lemon, juice only
30 g/1 oz. flour
1 tsp. salt
30 g/1 oz. butter
white pepper

1 tsp. chopped fresh thyme,
   or ½ tsp. dried
1 tsp. chopped fresh marjoram,
   or ½ tsp. dried
1 tsp. finely chopped chives
1 tsp. finely chopped parsley

To keep the scorzonera from discolouring, add the lemon juice to 2 liters/3½ pints of very cold water. Peel the scorzonera with a vegetable peeler and cut them in half, dropping the pieces into the water when peeled.

Put the flour in a large saucepan and stir in just enough of the lemon water to make a paste, then add the rest of the water. Add the scorzonera and half of the salt. Bring to a boil, stirring occasionally to keep the flour from forming lumps. Cook until tender - 10 to 12 minutes - and drain.

Melt the butter in a large, frying pan. Add the scorzonera, and shake the pan over the heat to coat it with the butter - about 1 minute. Then season with the remaining salt, the pepper and the herbs. Cook for 30 seconds longer to release the bouquet of the herbs. Serve immediately.

Fillet of Veal with Leeks and Shrimps in Salad Sauce

Serves 8

1.2 kilos/2½ lb. veal fillet
   in one piece, trimmed
60 g/2 oz. butter
1 large leek, trimmed, split and
   washed thoroughly to remove
   grit, and sliced
500 g/1 lb. shelled shrimps
salt and pepper

Salad Sauce
½ cup/4 fl.oz. white wine vinegar
½ cup/4 fl.oz. white wine
3 cups/2½ pints unsalted veal
   or chicken stock
1 cup/8 fl.oz. heavy cream
2 large lettuces, cored and washed
90 g/3 oz. quark
1 tbsp. Dijon mustard
salt and pepper

Preheat the oven to 200°C.

Brown the butter and sear the meat until it is sligthly browned on all sides. Remove from the heat and let the fillet cool off.

Blanch the leek rings 60 seconds in boiling water. Lightly cook the leek rings together with the shrimps in the same butter as the fillet - about 1-2 minutes.
Season with salt and pepper.

With a sharp knife, cut a slit along the side of the veal to make a pocket in the centre. Stuff the meat with the leekrings and shrimps and secure the stuffing by wrapping string around the meat.★

Place the parcel in a shallow oven pan and roast the meat 20-30 minutes depending on its thickness. Remove the meat from the oven and wrap it in foil. Let it rest 10-15 minutes before cutting the meat into thick slices.

Salad Sauce:
Reduce the vinegar over high heat to half. Add the wine and reduce this mixture to 1 tbsp. Pour in the stock and cook until it is reduced to about 1½ cups/12 oz. Add the heavy cream. Blanch one of the lettuce heads 60 seconds in boiling water. Place both of the lettuces in a blender or food processor with a little of the sauce, add the quark and run the blender/food processor 2-3 minutes. Add this mixture to the rest of the sauce together with the mustard. Season with salt and pepper.
Warm the sauce very carefully, it must not boil.

Suggested accompaniments: New baby potatoes and steamed carrots.

★ Loop the free end of a ball of string round the end of the meat and tie a knot. Without cutting the string, make successive loops at 3 cm(1¼ inch) intervals along the meat; tighten each loop by pulling the string as you go. Sesure the parcel by bringing the string under the entire length of the joint and knotting the free end.

Beef Patties with Onions

Serves 4

500 g/1 lb. ground beef
2 tbsp. butter
2 large onions, sliced
2 tbsp. flour

1 cup/8 fl.oz. potato water
  or water
1 cup/8 fl.oz. milk
salt and pepper

Form the meat into 4 patties. Brown half of the fat in a pan and fry the onions. Set aside.

Add the rest of the fat to the pan and heat until golden. Brown the patties on both sides, lower the temperature, and fry until done, about 3 minutes on each side. Remove the patties from the pan and set aside.

Stir the flour into the fat and cook until well browned, scraping in all the sediment. Gradually stir in the milk and then the potato water/water until the gravy reaches the right consistency. Remember, gravy is always thickened after being removed from the heat. A few drops of gravy browning or soy sauce may be added for additional color. Season with salt and pepper.

Arrange the onions rings on top of the patties and serve with boiled potatoes and cucumber salad. (see page 68) Serve the gravy separately.

Paris Steak Tartare

Serves 4

4 slices of white bread
300 g/¾ lb. lean ground beef
1 tbsp. finely chopped onion
1 tbsp. capers
salt, pepper
30 g/1 oz. butter

Garnish
4 egg yolks
4 onion rings
1 onion, finely chopped
4 tbsp. grated horseradish
a bunch of watercress

Combine the meat with the finely chopped onions, capers, salt and pepper. Spread the meat on the bread. Melt the butter and placing the meat side down first, quickly brown the meat, 2-3 minutes. The meat should be rare. Turn the bread over when the meat side is done and fry 1 minute. Turn off the heat and let the sandwich rest for a few minutes.

Place an onion ring in the center of each sandwich, meat side up, and place an egg yolk in the onion ring, or place an egg yolk in half of an egg shell. Place horseradish, finely chopped onion, and watercress decoratively around the egg yolk. Serve with salt and coarsely ground pepper straight from the mill.

Veal Birds

Serves 4

750 g/1½ lb. lean veal,
    cut in 8 thin slices
salt and pepper
8 strips of pork fat (if unavailable,
    use butter or bacon)
1 large onion, fincly chopped

flour
butter for frying
1½ cups/12 fl.oz. water or stock
1 cup/8 fl.oz. light cream
    flour for thickening

Sprinkle the meat slices with salt and pepper. Place a strip of pork fat/butter and some of the chopped onion on each piece. Roll the meat and tie with cotton string. Dredge with flour.

Brown the "birds" on all sides in the butter in a Dutch oven, or a large heavy-bottomed pot. Add the water or stock, cover, and simmer for about 60 minutes or until tender.

Remove the "birds" from the pot and keep warm. Add the cream. Bring to the boil and thicken with flour. Season with salt and pepper.

Return the "birds" to the sauce and heat them thoroughly before serving on a deep platter with mashed or boiled potatoes.

Veal Fricassee

Serves 4

1 kilo/2 lb. veal, shoulder or
   brisket
3 tsp. salt per liter of water
3-4 carrots, chopped
5-6 leeks, washed thoroughly to
   remove all grit, and chopped
1 cauliflower, cut into
   small florets
250 g/½ lb. shelled peas
   bouquet garni of leek tops and parsley

Sauce
3 tbsp. butter
3 tbsp. flour
½ liter stock
1 bunch parsley,
   finely chopped

Put the meat in a pot and pour on enough water to just cover. Bring to a boil and skim the broth. Add the vegetables, except the cauliflower and peas. Add the bouquet garni. Remove the vegetables when they are tender. Simmer the meat until done, about 1 hour. Cut the carrots and leeks into smaller pieces. Cook the cauliflower and peas in a little of the broth.

Sauce:
Melt the butter and stir in the flour. Add the strained broth gradually. Boil the mixture for a few minutes and season with salt and pepper. Place all the vegetables in the sauce and heat 5 minutes.

Slice the meat and arrange on a hot platter. Pour the sauce over. Sprinkle with finely chopped parsley.

Suggested accompaniment: New potatoes

Lamb fricassee can be made with this recipe. Use shoulder of lamb and cook it for 75 minutes.

These picturesque houses are located on the main street of Møgeltønder, which is near the home of the youngest Danish prince and his wife. The prince, who has an agricultural education, is the owner of Schackenborg, a manor house with a large farm acreage.

Lamb

Rack of Lamb

Serves 6

750 g/1½ lb. racks of lamb, each
   with 6 cutlets, chine bones
   removed, bone tips shortened by
5 cm/2 inches, trimmed of fat
1 small onion, finely chopped
2 garlic cloves, finely chopped

1 bunch of parsley, finely chopped
1 tsp. salt
freshly ground black pepper
½ cup/4 oz. white wine
1 tsp. cornflour

Preheat the oven to 220°C.

Mix together the onion, garlic, parsley, ½ tsp. salt and some pepper. Spread this mixture on the outer, fleshly side of the racks.

Place the meat on a rack in a roasting pan, the parsley side up. Roast for 25 minutes, then add the wine and ½ cup/4 oz. of water to the roasting pan and return the meat to the oven until the crusts are turning dark round the edges - about 20 minutes. The meat will still be slightly pink in the center; cover the racks with foil and roast them for an additional 15 minutes if you like lamb more thoroughly cooked.

When the meat is cooked, transfer it to a warmed plate. Skim off the fat from the cooking liquid, and boil the liquid rapidly to reduce it slightly. Mix the cornflour with 1 tablespoon of water and stir it into the pan. Continue cooking over medium heat until the gravy thickens - 2 to 3 minutes. Season the gravy with the remaining salt and some black pepper. Slice the racks into cutlets and serve with gravy, new potatoes and green beans.

Leg of Lamb Stuffed with Vegetables

Serves 10

2 kilo/4 lb. leg of lamb, trimmed
   of fat and boned
2 tbsp. oil
1 large carrot, cut into thin strips
1 large courgette, cut into thin strips
1 large yellow squash,
   cut into thin strips
½ cup/4 oz. dry sherry
1 tsp. salt

freshly ground pepper
1 tbsp. fresh thyme, or 2 tsp. dried
¼ liter/8 fl.oz. unsalted brown
   or chicken stock
2 tbsp. finely chopped shallot
   or onion
1½ tbsp. cornflour, mixed
   with 2 tbsp. water

To prepare the stuffing, heat 1 tablespoon of oil in a large casserole over medium heat. Add the carrot, courgette and squash, and cook the vegetables until the carrot is just tender - about 3-4 minutes. Remove from the heat and pour in 2 tbsp. of the sherry.

Preheat the oven to 170°C. Open the boned leg of lamb and sprinkle with salt and pepper and half the thyme. Spread the stuffing over the leg of lamb and roll it up. Tie the leg of lamb with string to secure it.

Pour the remaining oil in the casserole. Add the lamb roll and brown it over high heat - 2 to 3 minutes. Put the casserole into the oven and roast the lamb until it is tender - about 1 hour. Transfer the roast to a serving platter and set it aside to rest in a warm place.

Skim off the fat and set the casserole on the stove top over low heat. Add the stock, the remaining thyme, the shallot or onion and the remaining sherry to the casserole, then scrape the bottom to dissolve the caramelized roasting juices. Increase the heat and boil until about one third remains - 7-10 minutes. Reduce the heat and whisk in the cornflour mixture. Cook the sauce, stirring continuously, until it has thickened - about 1 minute. Season with salt and pepper. Cut the roast into slices. Pour the sauce into a sauceboat and serve it separately.

Suggested accompaniment: Peas and mashed potatoes

Lamb with Dill

Serves 4

500 g/1 lb. lean lamb
  (from the leg
  or loin) trimmed of fat and cut
  into 2.5 cm/1 inch cubes
1 tsp salt
1 small onion, quartered
2 fresh dill sprigs
1 bay leaf
4 black peppercorns
250 g/8 oz. potatoes, peeled
  and quartered

Dill Sauce
½ liter/16 fl.oz. stock
3 tbsp. chopped dill
30 g/1 oz. butter
3 tbsp. flour
1 egg yolk

Place the lamb in a casserole and cover it with cold water; add ½ tsp salt. Bring the water to boil and skim off the scum. Add onion, dill sprigs, bay leaf, peppercorns, and potatoes, then cover and simmer for 45 minutes or until very tender. Remove the potatoes when they are done, about 15-25 minutes.

Sauce: Strain the stock, there should be 2 cups/16 fl.oz. With a fork, cream the butter and flour together. Add this butter ball to the stock and when it has dissolved, cook 5 minutes. Add the dild, the cooked potatoes and salt and pepper. Mix 2-3 tablespoons of the warm sauce with the egg yolk. Add this mixture to the warm sauce. The sauce should not boil after this point.

Suggested accompaniment: Peas and baby carrots

Venison

Venison Fillet with Cherry Sauce

Serves 6-8

1.2 kilo/2½ lb. venison fillet
from the haunch, trimmed
2 tbsp. oil

Cherry Sauce
500 g/1 lb. fresh or canned
cherries, pitted
4 tbsp. red wine or sherry vinegar
½ liter/2½ pints unsalted brown
or chicken stock
200 g/7 oz. butter

Preheat oven to 200°C.

Sear the meat in hot oil until it is well browned on all sides, 3-5 minutes. Place the meat in a shallow oven pan and roast 20-30 minutes depending on the thickness. Remove the meat from the oven and wrap in foil. Let it rest 10-15 minutes before cutting the meat into thick slices.

Sauce: Reduce the vinegar to half over high heat. Add the stock and cook until it is reduced to about 1½ cups/12 fl.oz. Whisk in the butter a little at a time until the sauce is thick and shiny - about 1 minute. Add the fresh/canned cherries and heat them in the sauce.

Suggested accompaniment: Mashed parsnips and steamed spinach

Poultry

Tartlets with Asparagus and Chicken - as a first course

Serves 6

12 tartlets:
175 g/6 oz. flour
90 g/3 oz. butter
1 egg

Filling
3 tbsp. butter
3 tbsp. flour
½ liter/8 fl.oz. chicken broth
  (see page 20)
2 egg yolks
250 g/8 oz. canned asparagus tips
200 g/7 oz. cooked and diced chicken

Sift the flour into a mixing bowl. Add the butter and rub it into the flour with your fingertips until the mixture resembles fine breadcrumbs. Add the egg and form a dough. Knead briefly on a ligthy floured surface until smooth; do not overwork the dough or it will become oily and the baked pastry will be tough.

On a lightly floured surface, roll out the dough to a thickness of 5 mm/¼ inch. Cut out 12 circles with a glass and use them to line 6 cm/2½ inch deep tartlet tins. Prick the insides with a fork, then chill the tartlet cases for 30 minutes.

Preheat the oven to 220°C
Arrange the tartlet cases on a baking sheet and bake 5 minutes.

Filling: Melt the butter, stir in the flour and add the chicken broth a little at a time, stirring all the time. Add a little of the hot broth to the egg yolks and pour this mixture back into the broth. Do not let the sauce boil. Heat the asparagus and diced chicken in the sauce. Fill the warm tartlets and garnish with a few asparagus tips.

Roast Duck with Prunes and Apples

Serves 4

3 kilo/6 lb. duck, cavity washed
   and patted dry
salt and pepper
250 g/½ lb. pitted prunes
3-4 cooking apples, peeled
and quartered
1 onion, quartered
2 carrots, sliced
a sprig of thyme

Sauce
½ liter/16 oz. broth made
   from the wings, neck, giblets
salt
drippings
flour for thickening

Preheat the oven to 250°C.
Rub the inside of the duck with salt and pepper. Fill the cavity with apples and prunes. Close with a skewer or sew with cotton string. Pull the neck skin over the back and fasten with a skewer. Pat dry.

Place the duck upside down on a rack over a roasting pan. Brown it for 15 minutes. Turn and brown for another 15 minutes. Reduce the temperature to 175°C and sprinkle with salt and pepper. Pour off the fat from the pan and add water, together with the onion, carrots and thyme. Roast for 1¼ hours.

Boil the wings, neck, and giblets with chopped onion, carrots, celery, and thyme. Remove the duck from the oven and pour off the drippings. Let the drippings stand for a moment and skim off the fat.

Sauce: Pour the drippings into a small saucepan together with the strained broth, ½ liter/16 fl.oz. in all. Bring to a boil and thicken with flour mixed with a little water. Season to taste.

Pour a large spoonful of water over the duck and brown it at 250°C for 10-15 minutes with the oven vent open. Be careful it doesn't brown too quickly. Let the duck stand for at least 15 minutes before carving.

Suggested accompaniment: Glazed potatoes and red cabbage.

Braised Chicken with Cucumber Salad

Serves 4

1.5 kilo/3 lb. chicken	*Cucumber Salad*
a large bunch of parsley	1 large cucumber
salt and pepper	1 cup/8 oz. vinegar
75 g/2-3 oz. butter	2-3 tbsp. sugar
½ cup/4 oz. heavy cream	salt and pepper

Rinse the parsley well and remove the thickest stems. Rub the inside of the chicken with salt and pepper. Fill with parsley and a large pat of butter. Close with skewers. Heat the rest of the butter in a Dutch oven or a large heavy bottomed pot until golden brown. Brown the chicken evenly on all sides. Lower the heat and add half of the cream. Cover and braise the chicken for 65-75 minutes. Turn the chicken several times while cooking. Remove the chicken when a leg moves easily when it is wiggled. Add the rest of the cream and boil a few minutes. Season with salt and pepper.

Carve the chicken and arrange the meat on a warmed platter. Spoon some of the sauce over and serve the rest separately.

Cucumber Salad: Wash and dry a large cucumber thoroughly. If it is a spring cucumber the green rind may be left on, but late in the season, when the rind is thicker and harder, it is best to peel the cucumber. Cut the cucumber into very thin slices with a sharp knife. Mix the water and vinegar, and sweeten to taste.

Add the cucumber slices and sprinkle with pepper. Let stand for an hour or so before serving. Lemon juice can be used instead of vinegar.

Squab Breasts with Shallot-Cream Sauce

Serves 4

4 pigeon squabs, necks reserved, giblets discarded
½ tsp. salt
1 cup/8 fl.oz. white wine
2 onions, coarsely chopped
1 carrot, sliced in 5 mm/¼ inch rounds
2 garlic cloves, crushed
10 black peppercorns, crushed
1 tsp. fresh thyme, or ½ tsp. dried
15 g/½ oz. butter
½ onion, finely chopped
2 tbsp. heavy cream
2 tbsp. brandy
freshly ground pepper
1 tbsp. oil

To remove the squab breasts, cut the skin between the legs and breast and bend the legs down to the cutting surface. Remove each breast with its breastbone intact by cutting through the rib cage and round the wing socket. Sprinkle a little salt over the skin side of the breasts and put them in the refrigerator.

Cut up the back legs, wings and necks. Heat a large casserole over medium heat. Brown the chopped bones, (be careful that they don't burn,) until they are well browned and the bottom of the pan is lightly caramelized, 10-15 minutes.

Deglaze the casserole with wine. Add the onions, carrots, garlic, peppercorns, and enough water to just cover the bones. Bring the liquid to the boil over medium-high heat, skim off the impurities, and add the thyme. Reduce the heat to medium-low and simmer the stock for 30 minutes. Add ½ liter/16 fl.oz. of water and simmer for 1 hour more. Strain the stock into a small saucepan and discard the solids. Reduce the stock over medium-high heat to 1½ cups/12 fl.oz.

Preheat the oven to 200°C.

Sauce: Melt the butter in a saucepan over medium heat and cook the onions until they are translucent - about 3 minutes. Whisk in the cream and cook for 1 minute. Pour in 1 cup/8 fl oz. of the stock and simmer a few minutes, whisking constantly. Add the remaining stock and the brandy. Simmer for an additional 15-20 minutes, stirring occasionally, until the sauce has thickened slightly. There should be about 1 cup/8 fl.oz. of the sauce. Stir in the remaining salt and some pepper.

While the sauce is simmering, heat the oil in a large saucepan over high heat. Fry the squab breasts, skin side down for 3 minutes on each side of the breasts. Place the saucepan in the oven and roast the breasts skin side up for 6-8 minutes. Remove the breasts and let them stand for 3 minutes. With a small knife, cut each breast off the bone in one piece. Then cut the breast against the grain into thin slices. Arrange the slices on individual plates and spoon some sauce around them. Pass the rest of the sauce separately.

Suggested acompaniment: Peas and potatoes.

Salted Duck

Serves 6

The duck is salted in brine for 48 hours before it is cooked.

2½ kilo/5 lb. duck	15-20 g/½ oz. allspice
5 liters/5 quarts water	15-20 cloves
800 g/1½ lb. salt	6-10 bay leaves
90 g/3 oz. brown sugar	

Boil the water and dissolve the salt and sugar in the hot water. Add the allspice, cloves and bay leaves. When this mixture is cool, pour it over the duck and let stand in a cool place 48 hours. Pour off the water, place the duck in a large pot and cover with fresh water. Place a bouquet garni of leek tops and parsley and chopped vegetables in the pot and simmer gently for 1¼-1½ hours.

Suggested accompaniments: Potatoes sprinkled with chopped parsley, melted butter and vegetable.

Roast Pheasant

Serves 4

2 young pheasants, about 750 g/
1½ lb. each, cleaned
salt and pepper
30 g/1 oz. slab bacon, cut in 4
  pieces,or 2 slices of bacon halved
2 garlic cloves, peeled
2 bay leaves

2 sprigs of fresh thyme
1 tbsp. butter
2 carrots, cut in 5 mm/¼ inch
  thick slices
1 large onion, coarsely chopped
½ cup/4 fl.oz. dry white wine
1 cup/8 fl.oz. chicken stock

Sprinkle the pheasants with salt and pepper inside and out. Place two pieces of bacon and a garlic clove inside each bird with a bay leaf and a thyme sprig. Tie the legs together with string.

Preheat the oven to 180°C.

Melt the butter in a Dutch oven or a large heavy bottomed pot over moderate heat. Add the carrots and onion and cook, stirring frequently, until lightly browned, then remove with a slotted spoon.

Add the pheasants to the pan and brown quickly on both sides, then return the vegetables to the casserole and position the birds on top, lying on their sides. Add the wine and cook 30 minutes on top of the stove, then cover with foil and the lid. Place in the oven for 20 minutes.

Remove the casserole and turn the birds over; replace the foil and lid and continue cooking 15 minutes longer or until the juices run clear when the birds are pierced with a sharp knife. Remove from the oven and let the birds stand 10 minutes before carving.

Add the chicken stock to the pan drippings and cook 1 minute. Strain, pressing some of the cooked vegetables through the strainer with the back of a wooden spoon. Skim the fat from the surface before serving.

Suggested accompaniment: Cranberry sauce, waldorf salad and glazed potatoes

Open sandwiches

The coast of Denmark stretches for a length of 7300 kilometers. Scenes like this can often be seen while driving along the coast. Greenland, once under the rule of Denmark, but now an independent nation, supplies both Denmark and the world with shrimps, salmon and halibut.

The Danish open sandwiches (smørrebrød) are the most famous feature of the Danish kitchen. These delicious sandwiches are not found anywhere else, not even in the neighbouring countries of Norway and Sweden. There are hundreds of variations and new ones are constantly being composed.

Open sandwiches can be simple, "flat" sandwiches that adults as well as children take to work and school every day. Or they can range to the gloriously colorful compositions "piled high", so generously that one or two of them will be sufficient as a meal at a restaurant.

Danish open sandwiches are usually enjoyed with a glass of beer and on special occasions, aquavit, also a specialty of Denmark.

The garnish is a very important part of the sandwiches, so don't forget to decorate the sandwiches exactly as described.

Most Danish lunches start with fish, or more correctly, with herring. With the herring usually an aquavit (snaps) is drunk. There are many kinds and variations of herring, here are just a few.

Pickled Herring

Serves 4

3-4 large salt herrings	2 tbsp. water
1 cup/16 oz. vinegar	10 whole cloves
4-6 tbsp. sugar	1 bay leaf
1 small onion, finely chopped	10 whole peppercorns

Clean, skin and bone the herrings (see fried herring, page 37) and soak them 2-4 hours in cold water. Taste the herrings and if they are still too salty, soak them overnight.

Boil the vinegar, sugar, onion, water, cloves, bay leaf, and peppercorns. When the sugar is dissolved, pour the mixture into a bowl and refrigerate overnight. Rinse the herrings, cut them into 2.5 cm (1 inch) slices and marinate them for 24 hours before serving.

Drain the herring pieces before placing them on buttered bread. Or serve the herring in a bowl directly on the table decorated with thin raw onion slices and sprigs of fresh dill. Let the guests make their own open faced sandwich.

Herring Salad

Serves 4-6

2 salt herrings
2 small apples, peeled, cored, and cut into small pieces
2 cups/16 fl.oz. cooked beets, finely chopped
1 small onion, finely chopped

2-3 small dill/sour pickles, finely chopped
2 hard-boiled eggs, chopped
90g/3 oz. mayonnaise with ½ tsp. mustard

Place the salt herrings in a bowl of cold water to cover.
Soak for 2 hours. Drain and cut them into small pieces. Place the pieces in a mixing bowl together with the apples, beets, onions and pickle. Carefully stir in the mayonnaise/mustard mixture. Toss well. Chill for 2 hours.

Remove salad from refrigerator 45 minutes before serving. Toss again, sprinkle with chopped eggs, and serve.

Curry Herring

Serves 4

2-3 large pickled herrings

Dressing
1 cup/8 oz. low-fat sour cream
60 g/2 oz. mayonnaise
1½ tsp. curry powder
1 tsp. sugar
½ tsp. salt

Dice the herring. Combine the dressing. Fold in the fish.
Place the curry herring on dark buttered bread and garnish with
chopped hard-boiled egg and cress.

Egg with Caviar and Tomato Wedges

Arrange slices of hard-boiled egg on half slices of buttered dark
rye bread. Place a generous spoonful of caviar on each and garnish with one or two tomato wedges.

Shrimp Sandwich

Put a fresh leaf of lettuce on buttered white bread and top
abundantly with cold, boiled shrimps. Garnish with a sprig of dill
and a lemon wedge. Place freshly ground pepper on the table, so
each guest can take as much or little as he likes. Mayonnaise can
also be placed on the table, if a guest wishes to put some on his
sandwich.

Smoked Herring - Sun over Gudhjem

The smoked herring should be room temperature before skin-
ning. Cut off the head and tail fins. Split open and remove the
bones by placing the herring skin-side up, pounding it lightly
along the back. Now carefully peel off the skin, starting at the
tail. Turn the herring over and lift the bones out carefully. Arrange the fillets on dark buttered bread. Place a raw onion ring
in the middle of the sandwich and put an egg yolk inside it. Garnish with finely diced chives and radishes.

Smoked Salmon

Danish smoked salmon is world famous. A slice or two of salmon on buttered sourdough bread or white bread with just freshly ground pepper can be eaten at lunch together with other sandwiches or served as a first course on festive occasions.

Smoked Greenland halibut meat is white and does not have the same soft consistency as salmon, but it can be used in the same way as smoked salmon. Garnish with a sprig of dill.

Smoked Salmon or Greenland Halibut with Scrambled Egg

Place a piece of freshly smoked salmon on buttered white bread, and on top of that, diagonally across the bread, a strip of cold scrambled egg. Garnish with finely chopped dill.

Smoked Eel and Scrambled Egg

Cut smoked eel in 5 cm/2 inch pieces. Remove the skin and back bone. Put enough pieces of the eel on a piece of buttered dark rye bread to cover it completely. Top with slices of cold scrambled egg and sprinkle with chives.

Fried Fish Fillets with Homemade Remoulade

As the fried fish fillet (see page 30) should be served warm, do not place it on the bread as this would melt the butter. Serve buttered bread on the plate next to the fish or better yet, on a separate plate. Serve with remoulade (see page 30)

If the fillets are cold, place the fillet on buttered dark rye bread and garnish with remoulade and a lemon wedge. As an alternative the fish fillets could be garnished with a spoonful of caviar or some shrimps.

Fish Cake Sandwich

Slices of cold fish cakes (see page 35) can be used in the same way, just don't put caviar or shrimps on them. Garnish with cress.

Liver Paté (Liverwurst)

500 g/1 lb. pork liver	1 small onion, coarsely chopped
200 g/7 oz. lard or margarine	1 tsp. salt
2 tbsp. flour	¼ tsp. pepper
1 cup/8 fl.oz. milk or light cream	a pinch of cloves
1 egg	30 g/1 oz. anchovy fillet (optional)

Preheat the oven to 200°C.

Mix all the ingredients in a blender or food processor until the liver is reduced to a coarse purée. Pour this mixture into a greased oven-proof terrine. Cover the terrine with lightly oiled foil and bake for 60 minutes, removing the foil the last 20 minutes.

Put thick layers of cold paté on dark rye bread. Place a small dish on the table with cucumber salad (see page 68) or sliced red beets (see page 33) so that each quest may put some on top. Don't do it until the last minute, however, as the cucumber, red beets and liver paté may become soggy.

As an alternative pieces of crisp, fried bacon and lightly fried, thinly sliced mushrooms can be served on top of the warm paté.

Aspic or Jellied Consommé

1½ cups/12 fl.oz. strong, clear consommé	port wine (optional)
1 package (8 g/1 oz) powdered gelatin	

Heat the consommé and sprinkle with powdered gelatin. When the gelatin is dissolved, add a little port wine. Pour into one large or several smaller molds.

Refrigerate to jell. To serve, loosen the aspic around the edges.

Dip the mold a second in boiling water and unmold the aspic. Slice in strips.

The Veterinarian's Evening Sandwich

Place one or two thick slices of liver paté on buttered dark rye bread, a strip of aspic (see page 78) and two slices of salted veal (see page below) on top of the paté. Garnish with raw onion rings and some cress.

Salted Veal

1 kilo/2 lb. rump of veal

Brine
200 g/7 oz. coarse salt
3 tbsp. brown sugar
per liter/2 pints of water

Place the veal in a bowl and measure the amount of water needed to cover it.

Dissolve the salt and sugar in the water and pour the brine over the meat. Refrigerate for 2-3 days.

Place the meat in a large pot and cover with fresh water. Simmer gently for 30-45 minutes.

Chill the meat and slice before serving. Salted veal may also be served with just aspic and thin slices of raw onion.

Ham with Italian Salad

Italian salad
1 small diced carrot
6 stalks of asparagus,
cut into small pieces
slightly salted water

1 cup/8 oz. frozen peas
½ cup/4 oz. mayonnaise
2 tbsp. sour cream
salt, pepper

Cook the carrot and asparagus until just tender in the lightly salted water. Add the peas and bring the water to boil. Drain the vegetables and chill.

Mix the vegetables with the mayonnaise and sour cream, and season with salt and pepper.

Place a lettuce leaf on buttered dark rye bread. Place a slice of ham and a tablespoon of the Italian salad on top of the ham. Garnish with tomato wedges and cress.

Pork Tenderloin

Fry thick slices (2 cm/1 inch) of pork tenderloin in butter 2 minutes on each side. Sprinkle with salt and pepper. Fry slices of onion over a very low heat until they are tender and brown. Place one or two pieces of meat on buttered dark rye bread. Top with onions and if you wish, a fried egg.

Cold Roast Pork

Place thin slices of cold roast pork (see page 39) on buttered dark rye bread. Place a tablespoon of cold red cabbage on top (see page 42) and garnish with a thin slice of orange. If there are any crisp pieces of rind left over, place them on top.

Chicken Salad

1 cup/8 oz. of cooked or roasted chicken, diced	*Garnish* tomato wedges
150 g/5 oz. mayonnaise	cress
100 g/3 oz. cooked mushrooms, sliced	fried bacon
2 small stalks of celery, diced	
1 tbsp. lemon juice	
1 tsp. curry power	
salt and pepper	

Mix all the ingredients for the salad. Place a lettuce leaf on either buttered dark rye bread, or buttered toasted white bread and garnish with tomato wedges, cress and one or two pieces of crisp fried bacon.

Tartare with Egg Yolk

Put freshly ground, very lean raw beef on a piece of dark rye bread, forming the meat in the shape of the bread. Arrange an onion ring in the center of the beef and place an egg yolk in the center of the onion ring. Garnish with finely chopped onions, capers and freshly grated horseradish. Serve with salt and coarsely ground pepper from the mill.

Boiled Breast of Beef

Put slices of boiled breast of beef on dark buttered bread. Decorate with 1 tablespoon of pickles (relish) and shredded horseradish. Place a wedge of tomato right in the middle.

Roast Beef with Remoulade, Onions, and Shredded Horseradish

Put slices of cold roast beef on dark buttered bread. Fry onions in deep fat until brown and crisp and spread a layer of these on the beef. Place a tablespoon of remoulade, shredded horseradish, a wedge of tomato and slices of pickle on top.

Cheese is often used as the final course in a lunch which may include herring in some form as a starter, followed by liver paté, cold cuts of different kinds of meat and poultry and various salads.

Strong (Old) Cheese with Aspic

Put a slice of strong cheese on buttered (with lard or butter) dark bread. Place a strip of aspic and raw onion rings on top and pour 1 tbsp. of rum over.

Blue Cheese with Egg Yolk

Place slices of blue cheese on buttered toasted dark bread. Place a raw onion ring in the middle and put an egg yolk in it.

Desserts

The magic of the beautiful Tivoli gardens has inspired many people over the years. When Walt Disney on a visit to Denmark in the early sixties visited Tivoli, he conceived the idea for the creation of his Disneyland.

A visit to Copenhagen is not complete without a meal eaten in Tivoli. You may choose the traditional sandwich piled high with fresh, hand shelled shrimps and a glass of aquavit, or you may prefer to visit one of the cosy cafés for a cup of coffee with a typical Danish pastry.

Red Berry Dessert with Cream

Serves 4

250 g/½ lb. rhubarb stalks, coarsely chopped
2 cups/16 oz. water
250 g/½ lb. red currants
250 g/½ lb. black currants

250 g/½ lb. fresh strawberries
250 g/½ lb. fresh raspberries
150 g/8 oz. sugar
4-5 tbsp. cornstarch

Accompaniment: Fresh cream

Put the rhubarb in a pot with the red currants, and half of the black currants. Simmer gently for 5-6 minutes. Strain the mixture. Return it to the pot and add the rest of the black currants together with the strawberries and sugar. Cook briefly before adding the raspberries. Bring to a boil and stir. Dissolve the cornstarch in a little cold water and mix it into the boiling hot mixture. Pour into a serving bowl and sprinkle a little sugar to keep skin from forming. Serve cold with cream.

Lemon Mousse

Serves 4

4 eggs
6 tbsp. suger
grated peel of 1 lemon

fresh lemon juice from 2-3 lemons
1 tbsp. powdered gelatine
1 cup/8 fl.oz. heavy cream

Whisk the egg yolks and sugar until thick and creamy. Whisk in the grated lemon peel together with the lemon juice.

Pour 2 tbsp. of water into a small saucepan. Sprinkle in powdered gelatine. Heat the mixture over low heat, stirring continuously until the gelatine has dissolved. Let it cool a little, then pour it into the lemon mixture.

Beat the egg whites and the cream in two separate bowls. First fold the egg whites into the egg mixture, then half of the whipped cream. Pour the mousse into four individual bowls. Refrigerate before serving. Decorate with the rest of the whipped cream.

Rhubarb Compote

Serves 6

500 g/1 lb. tender rhubarb,
coarsely chopped

¼ liter/8 fl.oz. water
150 g/8 oz. sugar

Cook a syrup from the water and sugar. Add the rhubarb pieces
and cook 5-6 minutes over a low heat. Remove from the heat and
transfer the rhubarb pieces carefully to a serving bowl. Reduce
the syrup slightly by cooking it for a few minutes before pouring
it over the rhubarb. Serve warm or cold.

This compote is a popular accompaniment to lamb and veal.

Rhubarb Trifle

Serves 4

a portion of rhubarb compote
8-10 macaroons
3-4 tbsp. port wine

1 portion of vanilla cream
(see fruit salad with vanilla cream,
page 87)

Place the macaroons in a bowl and pour the port wine over.
Cover with the rhubarb compote and refrigerate. In the mean-
time, prepare the vanilla cream. When the compote is cold, place
the vanilla cream on top.

This recipe can be used with other kinds of fresh fruit, strawberries, and raspberries. Sprinkle a little sugar over the fresh fruit.

Strawberry Dessert with Cream

Serves 4

750/1½ lb. strawberries,
    hulled
1 cup/8 fl.oz. water or
    rhubarb juice

4-6 tbps. sugar
3 tbsp. cornstarch

Cook the stawberries in the water until tender - 4-5 minutes. Stir in sugar. Dissolve the cornstarch in a little water. Pour it into the hot mixture, stirring constantly. Serve cold with cream.

Cold Applesauce Cake

Serves 6

1 kilo/2 lb. dessert apples,
peeled, cored and sliced
1 vanilla bean
a little water
6 tbsp. sugar

Dried Bread-Crumb Mixture
7-8 tbsp. sugar
6 slices of day old bread
for making crumbs★

5 tbsp. butter
4 large or 8 small macaroons

Garnish
1 cup/8 oz whipped cream
raspberry or strawberry jam

Boil the apples with the split vanilla bean and a little water. When the apples are soft, remove the pot from the heat, discard the vanilla bean, and stir in the sugar. Cool the applesauce.

★   *Dried Bread Crumbs*
    Preheat the oven to 250°C. Place 6 bread slices in one layer on a cookie sheet; bake until slices are crisp and dry but not browned. Break slices into large pieces and blend in a blender or food processor at high speed until reduced to fine crumbs. Or, place in a strong, clean paper bag; with rolling pin, roll to make fine crumbs.

Mix the sugar with the dried bread crumbs. Melt the butter and toast the bread crumbs until crisp and golden. Remove from the heat and add the crushed macaroons. Arrange alternating layers of applesauce and the fried bread-crumbs in a bowl, beginning and ending with the mixture. Top with whipped cream and place a few dots of jam on top of the whipped cream.

Fruit Salad with Vanilla Cream
Serves 6

1 tart green apple, quartered, cored and cut into 1 cm (½ inch) pieces

2 ripe peaches or nectarines, halved, stoned and cut into 1 cm (½ inch) pieces

1 pear, peeled, cored and cut into 1 cm (½ inch) pieces

250 g/¼ lb. blueberries, picked over and stemmed, or seedless grapes

3 tbsp. lemon juice

Cream:
2 egg yolks
1-2 tbsp. sugar
1 vanilla extract
1 cup/8 oz. heavy cream, whipped

Place the apples, peaches, pear and blueberries in a large bowl. Pour the lemon juice over the fruit and toss, then refrigerate the bowl.

Whisk the egg yolks, sugar and vanilla extract together. Fold the whipped cream into the egg mixture just before serving. Serve the fruit salad and the cream separately.

Rice Pudding with Hot Cherry Sauce

Serves 6

1 liter/1¾ pints milk	50 g/2 oz. blanched, coarsely
90 g/3 oz. short-grained rice	chopped almonds
½ tsp. salt	1½ cups/12 fl.oz. heavy cream,
1 tsp. pure vanilla extract	whipped

Bring the milk to a boil in a heavy-bottomed pot. Add the rice gradually , stirring constantly. Cook the mixture for 50 minutes. Stir frequently to prevent the mixture from sticking. Remove the pot from the heat and stir in the salt.

When the mixture is cold, stir in the vanilla extract and chopped almonds. Fold in the whipped cream.

Refrigerate before serving. Serve with hot cherry sauce.

Cherry Sauce:

½ kilo/1 lb. canned stoned cherries in their syrup	1/1½ tsp. cornstarch

Put the cherries and their syrup into a saucepan and bring to a boil. Dissolve the cornstarch in a little water. Pour into the boiling hot liquid, stirring constantly. Serve immediately.

Pancakes with Ice Cream

approx. 12 pancakes

200 g/8 oz. flour	½ liter/16. fl.oz. milk
1 tsp. sugar	grated peel of 1 lemon
¼ tsp. salt	3 tbsp. beer or water
3 eggs	butter for frying

Combine the flour, sugar, salt and grated lemon peel. Beat the eggs and mix them with the flour and a little of the milk. Whisk in the rest of the milk together with the beer, and beat until smooth.

Pour a little of the batter onto a well greased frying pan and tilt so that batter quickly covers the bottom of the pan evenly.

Cook until golden brown on one side, then turn and cook on the other side. (Toss like flapjack or use turner or spatula.)

Serve with ice cream. Each person takes a lump of ice cream and with the help of a fork, rolls the pancake so that it resembles a tube with ice cream inside. Alternatively these pancakes can be served with sugar and strawberry jam.

Copenhagen - a city of beautiful towers. Every architectural style is represented here, and the inspiration for them has been borrowed from all over Europe. The city hall tower is the tallest with its 105 meters. The city hall is also the meeting place for important visitors from all over the world. Here the guests are served the famous City Hall pancakes.

City Hall Pancakes with Crème Filling

These pancakes are served to all official visitors at the Copenhagen city hall at festive receptions hosted by one of the city's 6 mayors.

Crème

3 egg yolks
2 tbsp. icing sugar
2 tbsp. orange liqueur
1 tbsp. powdered gelatine
50 g almonds, blanched
    and coarsely chopped

30 g/1 oz. candied orange peel
1 cup/8 fl.oz. heavy cream,
whipped
icing sugar

a portion of pancakes

Beat the egg yolks and sugar well and add the liqueur.

Pour 2 tbsp. of water into a small saucepan. Sprinkle in powdered gelatine. Heat the mixture over low heat, stirring continuously until the gelatine has dissolved. Blend the gelatine mixture into the egg mixture. Stir in the chopped almonds and candied orange peel and carefully fold in the whipped cream. Roll the pancakes around the crème and sprinkle with icing sugar.

Baking

Bread is a very important part of the Danish open sandwich. Most of the sandwiches call for dark bread. Here are two recipes.

These breads are made with Danish products and the results may not be the same elsewhere. Just keep trying with a little more or less flour. This bread is a must and tastes wonderful. So keep trying until you get it just right.

Dark Rye Bread

Sourdough starter:
1 cup/8 oz. plain yoghurt
15 g/½ oz.(approx. one package) active dry yeast
1½ cups/12 oz. rye flour
1 tsp. salt

Dough:
sourdough starter
¾ liter/1½ pints water
900 g/1¾ lb. rye flour
1 tbsp. salt
melted butter

Combine the yoghurt, flour and salt in a bowl. Cover the bowl with plastic wrap and place in the refrigerator for three days until the dough begins to bubble. Dilute the sourdough starter with water. Add the rye flour and the salt. Cover with a dish towel and let the dough rest in a warm place until the next day.

Turn the dough onto a lighty floured surface and knead until smooth. Remove approx. 1 cup/8 oz. of the dough as a starter for the next bread. Put it in a clean container, cover with plastic wrap and place it in the refrigerator.*

* Always take a lump of dough each time you make this bread and put it in the refrigerator. This way you will always have a starter for the next bread you make. The starter will stay fresh for three weeks. It can be frozen for up to three months. Be sure to take it out one or two days ahead of time and thaw it in the refrigerator. After the starter is thawed, it should be left at least one day, before being used.

Brush a 2 liter/2 quart loaf tin with melted butter. Place the dough in the tin, cover with a dish towel and let the bread rise 4 hours in a warm place. Brush the bread with the rest of the melted butter. Place the bread in a cold oven. Set the temperature to 180°C and bake for 1½ to 2 hours.

Wrap the bread in a clean dish towel and cool on a baking rack. It is best, not to cut the bread until the next day.

Dark Rye Bread with Yeast

Three packages of dry active yeast or 50 g/2 oz. fresh yeast
3 cups/¾ quart lukewarm water
1 kilo/2 lb. rye flour

2 tsp. salt
2 tbsp. light molasses
1 cup/8 oz. wheat flour

Dissolve the yeast in a little of the water then add the rest. Stir in the rye flour, salt and molasses. Knead the dough with wheat flour until it doesn't stick to your hands. Put the dough in a greased 2-liters/2 quarts loaf tin, cover with a dish towel, and let it rise in a warm place for two hours.

Place the tin at the bottom of a cold oven. Turn the temperature to 175°C and bake for 1¾ hour.

Wait until the next day to slice the bread.

Danish Pastry

The Danish pastry is probably the next most famous feature of the Danish kitchen. There are many kinds of pastry to choose from, here are just a few.

Pastry Dough

This is the dough which many different kinds of Danish pastry are made from.

500 g/1 lb. flour
3 tbsp. sugar
1 tsp. salt
30 g/1 oz. fresh yeast

1 cup/8 oz. milk
1 egg
360 g/12 oz. butter

Sift flour and mix with sugar and salt. Dissolve the yeast in half of the milk. Add yeast, the rest of the milk and the beaten egg to the flour and sugar. Beat until smooth.

On a lightly floured surface, roll out the dough to a thickness of 1 cm (½ inch). Spread small pieces of butter on ⅔ of the dough. The butter must have the same consistency as the dough; if it is too soft it melts into the dough. Fold together into three layers like folding a napkin, first the part without butter. Roll out and fold again. Repeat three or four times

Leave in a cold place for 30 minutes.

Chocolate Buns with Vanilla Crème

1 portion pastry dough

Butter Filling
90 g/3 oz. butter
90 g/3 oz. sugar

Vanilla Crème
1 egg yolk
1 tbsp. sugar
1 tbsp. flour
¾ cup/10 fl. oz. milk
½ tsp. vanilla extract

Preheat the oven to 225°C.

On a lightly floured surface, roll out the dough. Spread with a paste made of butter and sugar. Cut into squares of 10X10 cm(4X4 inches). Place filling of vanilla crème in the middle, fold corners to the center, forming dough as a ball and place upside down on a greased baking sheet. Leave in a cold place to rise for 15-20 minutes, then brush with egg white and bake 10 minutes.

After baking spread with a frosting of icing sugar, cocoa and water.

Vanilla Crème: Beat the egg yolk with sugar, flour and milk. Cook over low heat while beating the whole time until thick. Remove from the heat and add vanilla extract; then cool, stirring occasionally.

Cock's Combs

(Hanekamme)

1 portion pastry dough
1 portion butter filling
(see chocolate buns)

1 portion vanilla crème
chopped almonds
sugar

Preheat the oven to 225°C.

Roll out dough, spread with butter filling and cut as in chocolate buns. Place filling across the middle and fold over. Press the edges firmly together and make 4-5 deep slashes in this side. Place on a greased baking sheet and let rise, brush with egg white and sprinkle with chopped almonds and sugar.

Crème Tarts

(Linser)

360 g/¾ lb. flour
200 g/6 oz. butter

3 tbsp. sugar
2 egg yolks

Crème Filling: (see page 94 chocolate buns)

Sift and mix flour and sugar, combine with the cold butter and egg yolks. Knead the dough lightly and let it rise in a cool place for about 20 minutes.

Preheat oven to 190°C
Roll the dough on a light floured surface to a thickness of 3 mm (⅛ inch). Using a 7.5 cm (3 inch) cutter, cut 18 circles and use these to line 6 cm (2½ cm) tartlets tins. Prick the insides with a fork, then chill the cases for 30 minutes.

Put a tbsp. of the cooled filling in each cup. Cover with a lid of the dough and firmly press the edges. Bake 15-20 minutes.

Danish Roll with Jelly

(Spandauere)

1 portion pastry dough
1 portion butter filling
(see chocolate buns)

1 portion vanilla crème
(see chocolate buns)

Preheat the oven to 225°C.

Roll out dough, spread with butter filling and cut as for chocolate buns. Place crème in the middle. Fold corners to the center and press down. Place on a greased baking sheet. Leave in a cold place to rise for 15-20 minutes, then brush with egg white and bake 10 minutes.

Spread with frosting of icing sugar and water and drop 1 tsp. of jelly in the center when cooled.

Layer Cake with Crème and Fresh Fruit

(Lagkage)

1 portion of tart dough or
1 portion of roulade dough
   (see page 97 and follow the
   instructions for baking)
1 portion of vanilla crème
   (see page 94)

fresh fruit such as bananas,
   strawberries, kiwi - but not
   apple, oranges, or pears
1 cup/8 fl.oz. heavy cream,
   whipped
frosting of icing sugar and
   water

Preheat oven to 200°C.

Roll out the dough very thinly and with a sharp knife cut three large circles of 24-25 cm (10 inches). Place on a greased cookie sheet and bake 5 min.

When the cakes are cool, spread first with vanilla crème and then place fresh or canned fruit on top. Place another cake on top and again spread vanilla crème and the rest of the fruit. Then place the last cake on top. Decorate the sides of the cake with whipped cream and spread sugar frosting on the top. Decorate with more fresh fruit or grated chocolate.

Medallions

(Medaljer)

1 portion of tart dough	icing sugar
1 portion of vanilla crème	water
(see page 94)	

Preheat the oven to 200°C.

Roll out the dough very thinly, cut into round 6-8 cm/2-3 inch circles with a glas or a pastry cutter. Place on a greased cookie sheet and bake 5 minutes.

Spread half of the circles with a frosting made of icing sugar and water and the other half with vanilla crème and put them together.

Roulade

75g/2½ oz. butter	100 g/3½ oz. flour
100 g/3½ oz. sugar	½ tsp. baking powder
2 eggs	

Filling:	*To decorate:*
jelly, marmclade, applesauce	whipped cream, or
or other fruit, or vanilla crème	frosting of icing sugar and water

Preheat the oven to 170°C.

Mix the butter and sugar together and add the eggs one at a time. Add the flour and the baking powder. Pour the mixture onto a baking sheet lined with baking papir that is folded at each corner so that it forms a barrier. This way the dough cannot run over the edge. Bake 10 minutes.

While the roulade is still warm, spread the filling all the way to the edge at three sides, leaving a margin of 2.5 cm (1 inch) free of the filling along one long edge. Roll up the roulade, starting with the long side which has been coated to the edge. Seal the ends by pressing them together. Place the roulade, seam side down, on a platter. Decorate with whipped cream or frosting of sugar and water.

Danish Butter Cake

275 g/9 oz. flour
175 g/6 oz. butter
50 g of fresh yeast/3 packages
  of dry active yeast
3 tbsp. heavy cream
1 egg
1 tbsp. sugar

Butter Filling:
5 tbsp. icing sugar
150 g/5 oz. butter

1 egg, beaten

Crème:
2 egg yolks
1 tbsp. sugar
3/4 cup/6 fl.oz. milk
2 tsp. flour
½ tsp. vanilla extract

Icing:
1 cup/8 oz. icing sugar
a little sherry or water

Sift the flour into a mixing bowl. Add the butter and rub it into the flour with your fingertips until the mixture resembles fine breadcrumbs.

Crumble the fresh yeast into the cream. Beat the egg and sugar into the yeast mixture and pour this mixture over the flour. Mix all the ingredients together quickly. Do not overwork the dough or it will become tough.

Vanilla Crème: beat the egg yolks with sugar, flour and milk. Cook over low heat while beating the whole time until thick. Remove from the heat and add vanilla extract; then cool, stirring occasionally.

Butter Filling: Cream sifted icing sugar and butter together to a smooth cream.

Preheat the oven to 225°C.
On a lightly floured surface, roll out half of the dough to a large circle about 25 cm/10 inches. Place the dough in a prepared tin. Spread the crème on the bottom.

Roll out the other half of the dough in a long rectangle and spread the butter filling on it. Roll the dough together and cut in slices. Lay the slices on the vanilla crème. Let the cake rise 30

minutes in a cool place. Brush the cake with egg and bake 30-40 minutes.

Icing: Mix the icing sugar with a little sherry or water to a thick icing. Put a dab on each circle.

Strawberry Tartlets

1 portion tart dough

250 g/½ lb. fresh strawberries,   5 tbsp. redcurrant jelly
    hulled and halved

Roll out the dough on a lightly floured surface to a thickness of 3 mm (⅛ inch). Using a 7.5 cm (3 inch) cutter, cut 18 circles and use these to line 6 cm (2½ inch) tartlet tins. Prick the insides with a fork, then chill the cases for 30 minutes.
    Preheat oven to 220°C.
    Bake the tartlet cases for 15 to 20 minutes, until they are golden brown. Remove from the oven, allow them to cool a little, then unmould them onto a wire rack set over a tray.
    Arrange the halved strawberries in the tartlet cases. To prepare the glaze, place the redcurrant jelly in a small pan with 1½ tbsp. of water. Stir over gentle heat until the jelly has melted. Using a pastry brush, paint a generous amount of warm glaze over the strawberries in each tartlet; reheat the glaze if it begins to set.

Christmas Goodies

Sugar and Spice Cookies
(Brunekager)

2 cups/16 oz. dark syrup
1 cup/8 oz. brown sugar
½ cup/4 oz. butter
1 tbsp. baking powder
1 cup/8 oz. almonds, blanched
   and skin removed

1 tsp. cinnamon
½ tsp. ground ginger
½ tsp. ground cloves
500 g/1 lb. flour
almonds for decoration

Mix syrup, sugar and butter and bring to a boil. Remove from the heat and stir in baking powder, almonds, cinnamon, ginger, cloves and flour. It may be difficult for all the flour to be absorbed. Wait until the dough has cooled, knead the dough until it has absorbed most of the flour and is not sticky. There may be some flour left over. Refrigerate 1-3 days.

Preheat the oven to 170°C.

Knead thoroughly on a baking board - use more flour if it sticks. Roll the dough out very thinly, cut into round cookies with a glass or cookie cutter and place on a greased cookie sheet. Brush with egg white and decorate with half an almond. Bake 5-10 minutes.

Vanilla Rings

250 g/8 oz. flour	½ cup/4 oz. almonds, blanched,
200 g/7 oz. butter	skin removed and finely chopped
150 g/5 oz. sugar	1 tsp. vanilla extract
1 egg	

Work all the ingredients together and let the dough rest for 20 minutes.

Preheat the oven to 190°C.
   Put the dough into a piping bag fitted with a 1 cm (½ inch) star nozzle. Pipe the dough on to a lightly greased baking sheet, cut the dough into small pieces and form into small rings.
Bake until lightly brown - 3-5 minutes.

Christmas Crullers

(Klejner)

2 eggs	70 g/2½ oz. melted butter
250 g/½ lb. flour	grated rind of 1 lemon
90 g/3 oz. sugar	fat or oil for frying
1½ tbsp. heavy cream	

Mix egg, flour, sugar, cream, butter and grated rind into a smooth dough. Let the dough rest 1 hour or more before rolling it out very thinly and cutting long, narrow strips, 12 cmX2.5 cm (5X1 inch) with slanting ends. Make a slit in the center of each strip, put one of the ends through the slit, making a knot in the center. Fry in hot deep fat until light brown and drain on paper. Do not allow crullers to touch each other while frying.

Christmas Doughnuts

(Æbleskiver)

These doughnuts, which are only eaten at Christmas time, are baked on top of the stove in a special pan with a hole for each doughnut. It is called an "æbleskive" pan.

250 g/½ lb. flour
½ tsp. salt
2 cups/16 fl.oz. buttermilk
1 tsp. baking powder

2 eggs, separated
1 tsp. sugar
butter for baking

Accompaniment: Icing sugar and jelly

Mix flour, salt and sugar. Beat the buttermilk with the egg yolk, and add the flour mixture. Add baking powder and fold in stiffly beaten egg whites. Heat the "æbleskive" pan and put melted butter in each hole. Pour batter into each hole, not quite filling them. Place over a low heat and turn quickly with a knitting needle when half done, 1-2 minutes. Let them cook 1-2 minutes on the other side. Serve warm with icing sugar and jelly.

Each person takes two or three "æbleskive" on their plate together with a tablespoon of icing sugar and a tablespoon of jelly. The "æbleskive" is first dipped in jelly and afterwards in sugar, then eaten with the fingers.

Glögg - Warm Red Wine Drink

This hot drink is usually served at Christmas together with "æbleskiver" or Christmas cookies.

1 bottle of red wine
3 thin strips of lemon rind
3 pieces of cardamom
4 whole cloves
a small piece of fresh ginger
1-2 pieces (5 cm/2 inches)
   of cinnamon

½-1 cup/4-8 oz. raisins
30 g/1 oz. blanched, coarsely
chopped almonds
½-1 cup/4-8 oz. port wine

Pour one cup of the red wine into a casserole. Add the lemon rind and the spices. Bring the mixture to the point of boiling and simmer, without boiling, 10 minutes. Strain and add the rest of the red wine, raisins and almonds. Bring the mixture to the boiling point and remove from the heat. Add the port wine and serve immediately in a cup or glass with a spoon. This way the raisins and almonds can be eaten. Depending on how much money you want to spend or what you have in the house, a little brandy may be added.

Index

Index in Danish